Council of the
INSPECTORS GENERAL
on INTEGRITY *and* EFFICIENCY

Don't Let the Toolbox Rust:

Observations on Suspension and Debarment, Debunking Myths, and Suggested Practices for Offices of Inspectors General

Suspension and Debarment Working Group

Working Group Chairs

Inspector General Allison Lerner, National Science Foundation
Inspector General Steve Linick, Federal Housing Finance Agency

September 20, 2011

Table of Contents

Appendices

Introduction and Executive Summary

In light of Congress' continuing interest in ensuring that scarce federal funds are spent responsibly,[1] and the ready availability of suspension and debarment processes to protect those funds, the Council of Inspectors General on Integrity and Efficiency (CIGIE), Investigations Committee formed a working group -- which has been integrated into the Federal Fraud Enforcement Task Force, led by the Department of Justice (DOJ) -- to examine ways in which the use of these remedies can be increased.

As one of its first tasks, the Working Group informally surveyed the federal Inspector General (IG) community to gather basic information on suspension and debarment use and practices within the various Offices of Inspectors General (OIGs) with an eye toward identifying the extent to which these tools are used across the IG community, as well existing practices that agencies new to the process could emulate.[2] In general, the respondents indicated their belief that these remedies could be used more frequently and more effectively. Most suspensions and debarments rely on findings that are identified through indictments, criminal convictions, and civil judgments to establish the basis for action (collectively referred to in this report as "judicial findings"). Actions based entirely on the strength of the facts absent a predicate judicial finding (referred to as "fact based" suspension and debarment actions) are less frequent. The survey highlighted a need for all relevant communities involved in suspension and debarment -- the Suspension and Debarment Officials (SDOs), OIG staff (who provide information to support these actions), and DOJ attorneys (who may be involved in proceedings running parallel to the proposed action) -- to communicate and collaborate. The survey also highlighted the potential benefits from enhanced training and more effective referral practices in the IG community.

This report builds on the survey information summarized above. It is intended primarily to raise the profile of suspension and debarment within the IG community, and to identify practices that could assist OIGs in pursuing these remedies. To this end, the report features three sections. The first section provides basic background information about these remedies. The second section addresses certain misconceptions about suspension and debarment that may limit use of these actions: (1) that pursuing these actions necessarily jeopardizes contemporaneous judicial proceedings; (2) that they require a predicate judicial finding; and (3) that successful OIG

---

[1] *See generally* American Recovery and Reinvestment Act, Pub. L. No. 111-5, 123 Stat. 115 (2009) (containing heightened levels of oversight, transparency, and accountability); *see also, e.g.*, Hearings on Suspension and Debarment, House Committee on Oversight and Government Reform (February 26, 2009, March 18, 2010) (discussed further herein).

[2] This survey was intended to informally gather basic information about the IG community's suspension and debarment usage and practices. We note that 39 out of 73 OIGs responded to the survey (and not all 39 answered every question).

1

referrals can only be based upon investigative action, not audit or inspection activities. The third and final section identifies a number of suggested practices aimed at enhancing the use of these tools in the IG community, such as those pertaining to referral processes at certain OIGs, outreach and communication between relevant communities, and training.

Background on Government-Wide Suspension and Debarment

A Brief Primer

Government-wide suspensions and debarments are administrative remedies that federal agencies may take in order to protect taxpayer dollars from fraud, waste, abuse, poor performance, and noncompliance with contract provisions or applicable law.[3] Debarment ensures that for a defined period of time, the entire federal government will not do additional business with individuals and organizations that are not "presently responsible"-- i.e., those that have engaged in criminal or other improper conduct of such a compelling and serious nature that it would lead one to question their honesty, ethics, or competence.[4] Suspension is a preliminary action taken where there is a need to act to protect the integrity of a federal procurement or nonprocurement process before there is enough evidence to support a debarment proceeding. Although these remedies preclude the government from engaging in future business with the subject entity or individual (such as new contracts or nonprocurement awards, including grants or cooperative agreements), agencies may decide to continue existing awards or to terminate performance.[5]

There are essentially two types of suspensions and debarments: those which an agency may elect to pursue ("discretionary") and those which are automatic under law ("statutory"). Discretionary suspensions and debarments arise from the federal government's inherent authority as a purchaser and consumer of goods and services to limit the pool of those with whom it will do business to those who have demonstrated responsibility and integrity. Statutory debarments -- there are no statutory suspensions -- are created by Congress to further certain socio-economic goals. One such example is the automatic disqualification of any party convicted of a Clean

---

[3] On February 18, 1986, President Reagan issued Executive Order 12549, "Debarment and Suspension," to establish a government-wide debarment and suspension system covering the full range of federal procurement and nonprocurement activities, and to establish procedures for nonprocurement suspension and debarment actions.

[4] See Appendix A for an overview of causes for debarment.

[5] FAR 9.405-1(a) (explaining that "agencies may continue contracts or subcontracts in existence at the time the contractor was debarred, suspended, or proposed for debarment unless the acquiring agency's head or a designee directs otherwise"); 2 CFR § 180.315(a) [hereinafter NPR] (agencies "may [but are not required to] continue to use the services of an excluded person as a principal . . . if [they] were using the services of that person in the transaction before the person was excluded").

Water Act violation from receiving new federal awards for work to be performed in whole or in part at the facility that gave rise to the violation.[6] This report focuses only on discretionary suspensions and debarments.

Discretionary suspension and debarment actions are governed by the Federal Acquisition Regulation (FAR) at 48 CFR Part 9.4, which cover procurements, and by the Office of Management and Budget (OMB) Guidelines to Agencies on Governmentwide Debarment and Suspension (Nonprocurement) (NPR) at 2 CFR Part 180, implemented by agencies through supplementing adopting rules, which cover nonprocurement transactions such as grants, loans, or benefits. Suspension and debarment actions have government-wide reciprocal effect, meaning that if a company is suspended or debarred from doing additional business with one federal agency, it is also suspended or debarred from doing additional business with other federal agencies. These actions are undertaken only when they are found to be in the federal government's best interest, since suspension and debarment cannot be used as punishment.[7] Determining whether these remedies are in the federal government's best interest requires two basic inquiries: (1) whether cause exists to suspend or debar;[8] and (2) whether there is a need to protect the integrity of the federal government's procurement and nonprocurement award program.[9] A debarment's length is tailored to the seriousness of the underlying cause on which it is based, and generally does not exceed three years.[10] Suspension, as noted above, is preliminary and temporary. As a general rule, unless legal proceedings have been initiated, a suspension will not extend beyond twelve months (a suspension can last for the duration of proceedings that have been initiated).[11] In addition, SDOs have flexibility to lift a suspension when appropriate (e.g., if "present responsibility" issues have been alleviated).[12]

Increasing Suspension and Debarment Use Would Help Protect Federal Funds

Although there can be overriding and compelling justifications, an agency's reluctance or refusal to suspend or debar a non-responsible party often jeopardizes not only the integrity of that

---

[6] *See* Debarment and Suspension of Government Contractors: An Overview of the Law Including Recently Enacted and Proposed Amendments, Congressional Research Service (Jan. 20, 2011) (listing other statutory debarments).

[7] FAR 9.402(b); NPR Preamble, 68 Fed. Reg. 66541 (2003).

[8] *See* Appendix A for an overview of causes.

[9] The FAR and NPR each list a number of mitigating factors for the Suspension and Debarment Official (SDO) to consider. FAR 9.406-1(a) (1) – (10); NPR § 180.860.

[10] FAR 9.406-4(a)(1); NPR § 180.865(a).

[11] FAR 9.407-4(b); NPR 180.760(a). The Department of Justice can request a six-month extension in the absence of legal proceedings. FAR 9.407-4(b); NPR § 180.760(b).

[12] FAR 9.407-4(a).

agency's programs, but also the integrity of contract and financial assistance awards across the federal government. By contrast, a federal agency's vigorous and appropriate use of suspensions and debarments can help prevent future losses government-wide.

These issues were highlighted in congressional hearings in the last few years. In February 2009, the House Committee on Oversight and Government Reform held a hearing on the operation and use of the Excluded Parties List System (EPLS), which contains information for every suspended and/or debarred party. Federal agencies are required to consult the EPLS prior to awarding a contract or a grant or entering into other transactions. In his opening statement, the Committee Chairman noted that too often federal government agencies were not taking suspension and debarment actions even when causes for action clearly existed.[13] In March 2010, the Committee again held hearings on agencies' use of suspension and debarment and concluded that little had changed since the earlier hearing. In one instance, the Committee noted that two large corporations admitted they had submitted more than 100 false claims for reimbursement and agreed to pay $1.31 million to the federal government. However, the agency that awarded the contracts took no suspension or debarment action.[14] This left the agency's own programs at risk, as well as those of other agencies that might do business with the contractors. Then-Committee Chairman Edolphus Towns concluded that "[s]uspension and debarment can be an effective tool for federal agencies to ensure contractor performance. Unfortunately . . . the suspension and debarment tools often go unused, quietly rusting away in the procurement toolbox."[15]

The Working Group's survey results reflected a prevailing view within the IG community that these remedies could be used more often, echoing the above-mentioned views expressed by the former Committee Chairman.[16] When asked to identify possible factors influencing pursuit of these remedies, most respondents cited a general lack of awareness about suspension and debarment, including limited knowledge about the procedures/criteria associated with these actions, as well as concerns about the potential impact suspension or debarment proceedings

---

[13] Opening Statement of Chairman Edolphus Towns, House Committee on Oversight and Government Reform (February 26, 2009). The Committee's hearing followed issuance of a report by the Government Accountability Office (GAO) entitled "Excluded Parties List System, Suspended and Debarred Businesses and Individuals Improperly Receive Federal Funds" (February 2009).

[14] Opening Statement of Chairman Edolphus Towns, House Committee on Oversight and Government Reform (March 18, 2010), at 3.

[15] Id. at 1.

[16] The Working Group notes that a minority of survey respondents felt differently. These respondents felt that suspension and debarment were well used within their respective agencies. They cited strong relationships between the OIG and the agency's SDOs as contributing factors. One OIG explained that employment of a full-time OIG suspension and debarment professional contributed to effective suspension and debarment use within the agency. (See discussion of assignment of dedicated personnel in the Suggested Practices section below.).

might have upon contemporaneous civil or criminal proceedings (i.e., through premature disclosure of evidence). Hesitation by agency officials (whether due to resource concerns or simply from conservative approaches regarding the level of evidence needed) was also noted as a specific factor influencing pursuit of fact-based actions -- i.e., actions that are not based upon a judicial finding.

Each agency has different needs and may encounter varying and sometimes agency-specific obstacles to increased suspension and debarment use. Based on the results, of the survey the Working Group believes that one step toward enhanced use involves dispelling some common misconceptions about these remedies, as discussed in the next section of this report. The subsequent section, entitled "Suggested Practices," discusses other steps to enhance use of these tools such as: fostering ongoing dialogue between relevant communities (OIGs, SDOs, and DOJ); developing and presenting highly relevant and targeted training presentations to those communities; and expanding the use of effective practices, such as those practices pertaining to OIG referral preparation and tracking.

"Myth Busting" -- Addressing Misconceptions

Misconceptions regarding suspension and debarment may be affecting more frequent use of these remedies. The discussion below attempts to dispel three myths about suspension and debarment: (1) that contemporaneous civil or criminal proceedings will be compromised if suspension or debarment is pursued, (2) that suspension and debarment actions must be tied to judicial findings (conviction, civil judgment, or indictment), and (3) that referrals may not be based on OIG audits or inspections.

Effect on Contemporaneous Activities and Proceedings

The Working Group understands that some OIGs and prosecutors may resist seeking suspension and debarment, believing that doing so might result in sensitive investigative information or case theories being disclosed to the subject through the suspension and debarment process, thereby compromising contemporaneous investigations or judicial proceedings.[17] However, processes exist to protect contemporaneous proceedings while suspension and debarment actions are pursued. For example, while a notice of proposed debarment or suspension must inform the subject of the agency's stated ground(s) for taking the action, it need not disclose all of the agency's evidence.[18] Indeed, courts have elaborated that the suspension notice must contain

---

[17] Concerns about the effect on contemporaneous proceedings are more apt to arise with suspensions, rather than debarments. This is because debarments, for example, are more typically imposed after there has been a conviction or when the investigation has been completed.

[18] FAR 9.406-3(c)(2), 9.407-3(c)(1); NPR §§180.715(c), .805(b).

only enough information regarding the time, place and nature of the alleged misconduct to permit the subject to "get his ducks in a row" in order to meaningfully contest the suspension.[19] Requests for documents underlying a suspension may be denied if pending proceedings might be harmed through their disclosure.[20] Also, while the governing rules contemplate fact-finding hearings when material facts are in dispute, the applicable regulations *require* that requests for such hearings be denied -- at least for proposed suspensions -- if DOJ advises that contemporaneous proceedings would be prejudiced by disclosing evidence publicly.[21] Further, as a practical matter, OIG referrals need only provide enough information to satisfy the applicable evidentiary standard. For suspensions, only "adequate evidence" (similar to the threshold for a search or arrest warrant) of debarrable conduct need be introduced to support the proposed suspension. For instance, some OIGs have successfully obtained suspension actions by providing the SDO with only a copy of a search warrant affidavit that had previously been disclosed to the subject. No other evidence within the government's possession was provided, or needed, to support a suspension. The threshold is only slightly higher for debarments, which require that the claimed debarment ground be established by a "preponderance of the evidence" -- i.e., that it is "more likely than not" that the debarrable conduct occurred.

Perhaps the best way the relevant communities (OIGs, DOJ, SDOs, and others) can resolve their concerns about the impact of suspension and debarment on ongoing civil or criminal matters is to communicate frankly and continuously regarding all evidence sharing issues. Disputes may be avoided or minimized through active dialogue and a willingness to be flexible in the interest of maximum accommodation.[22] (See discussion of outreach between relevant communities under Suggested Practices discussed herein.)

Availability and Viability of Fact-Based Actions

Suspension and debarment actions are often, and appropriately, based upon the results of judicial findings, such as an indictment, information, conviction, or civil judgment for one or more

---

[19] *See ATL, Inc. v. United States*, 736 F. 2d 677, 686 (Fed. Cir. 1984); *Transco Security, Inc. v. Freeman*, 639 F.2d 318 (6th Cir. 1981), *cert. denied*, 454 U.S. 820 (1981).

[20] *See* NPR Preamble, 68 Fed. Reg. 66543 (2003) ("[t]he suspending official may have to review [sensitive] evidence [pertaining to an investigation] *in camera* and be unable to disclose the evidence to a suspended respondent"). *Cf.* 5 U.S.C. § 552(b)(7)(A) (Freedom of Information Act exemption protecting records, which, if disclosed, could reasonably be expected to interfere with a law enforcement proceeding). The concept of an *in camera* review, in which evidence is not disclosed to the respondent, is supported by the *ATL* and *Transco* cases, above.

[21] FAR 9.407-3(b)(2); NPR §180.735(a)(4).

[22] Full and open communication, of course, could be limited by rules pertaining to grand jury secrecy in certain circumstances.

integrity-related offenses.[23] However, as evidenced by the Environmental Protection Agency's (EPA) suspension of IBM in 2008 and the Small Business Administration's (SBA) suspension of GTSI in 2010, this is not the only path to exclude an irresponsible party from doing business with the government.[24] There are many occasions when protecting the government's interest warrants pursuit of "fact-based" actions, which do not rely on such a judicial finding. Results from the OIG survey showed that such actions are not very common. Respondents indicated that only 27% of suspension referrals and 24% of debarment referrals in FY 2010 were purely fact-based.[25]

According to the Working Group survey, pursuit of fact-based actions may be affected by agency concerns over potential difficulties associated with a fact-finding hearing, such as the time and resources that might be involved. Misunderstandings about the level of evidence needed to sustain an action that is not based on judicial findings, and (as earlier mentioned) concerns about the potential impact on contemporaneous proceedings might also play a role. More basically, though, many agencies and OIGs may mistakenly believe that suspension and debarment actions need always arise from judicial proceedings.[26]

In reality, the FAR and NPR contemplate fact-based actions by providing that debarment can be supported by a preponderance of the evidence[27] sufficient to establish, among other things:

- A particularly serious violation of the terms of a government contract, subcontract, or transaction, or

- Any other cause of such a compelling and serious nature that it affects present responsibility.[28]

---

[23] Such offenses include commission of any offense indicating a lack of business integrity or business honesty that seriously and directly affects present responsibility. FAR 9.406-2(a); 9.407-2(b); NPR §§180.705(b); .800(a).

[24] Regarding IBM, the EPA OIG uncovered adequate evidence that IBM executives on a bid team seeking an $84 million contract award may have received procurement sensitive information from certain EPA procurement officials. The collusion resulted in EPA improperly awarding a contract to IBM. Therefore, both of the requirements for suspension, adequate evidence and immediate need, were met by the facts alone here. The SBA suspended GTSI for improperly performing contracts that were set aside for small businesses. SBA did not rely upon an indictment or other judicial finding as evidence for this suspension.

[25] These percentages are based on the small number of survey respondents that provided sufficient information to permit a comparison. The actual rate of fact-based referrals could be lower.

[26] As noted earlier, survey respondents cited uncertainty and/or a lack of understanding about suspension and debarment as a leading reason why they believe these remedies are not used to a greater extent.

[27] A "preponderance of the evidence" means proof leading to the conclusion that a fact in issue is more probable than not. *See* FAR 2.101; NPR § 180.990.

[28] FAR 9.406-2(b)(1)(i), (c); NPR §§ 180.800(b), (d). A list of the causes for debarment that may be established factually (i.e., without a predicate judicial finding) can be found at FAR 9.406-2(b), (c); and NPR § 180.800(b), (c), (d); these causes are also summarized in Attachment A.

The latter category is especially broad and permits the SDO to debar an individual or entity for a wide variety of conduct indicating, for example, a lack of integrity or competency to handle federal funds. Additionally, the NPR also provides that suspensions and debarments may be based upon a "willful violation of a statutory or regulatory provision or requirement applicable to a public agreement or transaction."[29]

Likewise, suspensions may -- but need not -- flow from court findings. While an indictment alone can establish cause for suspension,[30] such action may also be appropriate based on other "adequate evidence" (again, a lower standard akin to probable cause) establishing a cause for debarment, including any cause so serious that it implicates present responsibility. There must also be an accompanying need for immediate action to protect the government's interest.[31]

Cause for a fact-based suspension or debarment can arise at any point during a contract or grant lifecycle and may be identified well before the final completion of an audit, investigation, or award close-out. Given that the purpose of suspension and debarment is to protect the government from doing further business with those not presently responsible, OIG and agency officials should be aware of the need and ability to act promptly when cause for a suspension or debarment action exists.

Referrals Arising from Audits and Inspections

Suspensions and debarments can also rest upon facts uncovered during OIG audits or inspections, in addition to those uncovered during investigations.[32] The OIG survey found that in FY 2010, only 1.5% of respondents' suspension and debarment referrals arose from non-investigative activities. Further, when asked "How often has your office recommended suspension and debarment as an audit recommendation," only 1 respondent answered "Regularly." Most respondents replied that they did so either rarely (23.1%) or never (69.2%). The response was even lower within the inspections context: 94.7% of respondents replied that they had never recommended suspension or debarment as the result of an inspection, with only 2 respondents (5%) indicating that they had.

The low rate of non-investigative referrals may be attributable, in part, to many audits' and inspections' focus on the internal operations of their agencies or on grantees that are predominately state and local government entities. Also, many OIGs do not have an inspection

---

[29] NPR § 180.700(b), 180.800(b).

[30] FAR 9.407-2(b), NPR § 180.700(a).

[31] FAR 9.407-1(b), NPR § 180.700(c).

[32] Process-wise, even where there is an investigation, the referral does not have to be made by the investigative component, but, if circumstances warrant, can be made by the OIG as a whole (or perhaps made through the Office of Counsel).

function, since one is not expressly required by the IG Act of 1978. The Working Group also notes that some OIGs may require audit and inspection units to refer fraudulent or improper activity discovered during the course of their work to the offices of investigations.[33] Nevertheless, externally-focused audits and inspections may present opportunities for suspension and debarment referrals since, as mentioned, the FAR and NPR permit these actions for any "serious or compelling" cause affecting "present responsibility," including contractual or regulatory violations as noted earlier.

For example, the SBA OIG included in an audit report a recommendation for a debarment based upon a finding that a company had made inaccurate statements to obtain admission to an agency procurement program.[34] An audit might also adequately document cause for suspension or debarment by showing significant or recurring internal control deficiencies that place federal funds in danger of misuse or misallocation. Reports of audits conducted pursuant to OMB Circular A-133 may be a good source of suspension and debarment referrals -- at least as they relate to non-public entities. These audits provide oversight of institutional management controls and financial practices and, unlike many OIG-conducted audits, offer a continuous look at a single institution. A series of A-133 audit reports can readily identify trends and persistent problems with particular awardees that may reflect upon "present responsibility."

Because non-investigative referrals are uncommon, some groundwork may need to be laid to help ensure their growth and success. In particular, focused training for auditors and inspectors on how their work can produce and support suspension or debarment opportunities might be beneficial. Also, many SDOs and other agency officials may be less familiar with these types of referrals than with those arising from investigative activities; hence, preliminary discussions between OIGs and agency staff concerning audit and inspection-based referrals may be advisable to avoid confusion and surprises.

Suggested Practices

The OIG survey responses revealed a number of suspension and debarment-related practices that could help boost the overall use and effectiveness of these remedies within the community. Practices the IG community may want to consider, as appropriate, are discussed below.

---

[33] This report should not be construed to discourage OIG auditors and inspectors from coordinating with, and making fraud referrals to, their offices of investigations. However, there may be instances in which such matters ultimately are not pursued as investigations, but present responsibility issues remain. In these cases, it would be appropriate for auditors and inspectors to pursue suspension or debarment referrals.

[34] Acceptance of VBP Group Into the 8(A) Program and Subsequent Contract Award by SBA, Report No. 8-16 (July 18, 2008), http://archive.sba.gov/idc/groups/public/documents/sba/oig_8-16.pdf.

Assignment of Dedicated Personnel within OIGs

OIG staffing considerations can affect the frequency with which suspension and debarment referrals are undertaken. Given the different sizes and structures of the various OIG offices, there is no standard approach to staffing that applies across the IG community. However, some OIGs provided information about staffing approaches they have followed to promote the pursuit of these remedies. The Department of Interior (DOI) OIG, for example, has a full-time debarment manager assigned only to suspension and debarment issues. This debarment manager has case-specific duties, trains DOI staff on suspension and debarment issues, and fits into a larger DOI/DOI OIG policy on suspension and debarment use. Along similar lines, Department of Homeland Security (DHS) OIG has designated two in-house suspension and debarment experts, one in the Office of Investigations who coordinates referrals, and one for policy matters. One survey respondent reported that its Office of Investigations had "also assigned an agent to work as the OIG's primary liaison on suspension and debarment and procurement and nonprocurement fraud matters" and that this individual is primarily responsible for making referrals to the agency. Insofar as resources permit, OIGs may want to consider similar staffing arrangements to support their suspension and debarment efforts. Such arrangements contribute to success by building in-house expertise as well as stable relationships with the agency suspension and debarment staff.

Identifying and Recommending Improvements to Agency Suspension and Debarment Programs

Another means by which OIGs might contribute to more frequent and effective suspension and debarment use is through internal audits and reviews to evaluate the efficacy of their agency's suspension and debarment system. This is a straightforward way to focus attention on suspension and debarment programs: namely, identifying deficient (or even non-existent) processes and shedding light on them to effect a positive change.

The Working Group survey and other materials indicate that at least ten OIGs have conducted such audits or reviews.[35] For example, Department of Commerce (DOC) OIG issued a January

---

[35] Examples of OIG reports addressing agency suspension and debarment practices include: Effectiveness and Enforcement of Suspension and Debarment Regulations in the U.S. Department of Agriculture, (USDA OIG August 16, 2010), http://www.usda.gov/oig/webdocs/50601-14-AT.pdf. Weaknesses in DOT's Suspension and Debarment Program Limit its Protection of Government Funds, (DOT OIG March 18, 2010), http://www.oig.dot.gov/library-item/5296; DHS' Use of Suspension and Debarment Actions for Poorly Performing Contractors, (DHS OIG February 2, 2010), http://www.dhs.gov/xoig/assets/mgmtrpts/OIG_10-50_Feb10.pdf; Audit of USAID's Process for Suspension and Debarment, (USAID OIG October 1, 2009), http://www.usaid.gov/oig/public/fy10rpts/9-000-10-001-p.pdf; Review of GSA's Suspension and Debarment Program, (GSA OIG December 20, 2007), http://www.gsaig.gov/auditreports/reports/A070105_1.pdf; Suspension and Debarment Process, (USPS OIG October 22, 1999), http://www.uspsoig.gov/FOIA_files/FA-AR-00-001.pdf. NRC OIG conducted an audit of its grant management program (Report OIG-09-A-16) that included a finding that the Agency lacked any regulation governing debarment and suspension for grant recipients. Audit of NRC's Grant Management Program (NRC OIG September 29, 2009), http://www.nrc.gov/reading-rm/doc-collections/insp-gen/2009/oig-09-a-16.pdf. HUD OIG,

2011, memorandum to the Department's Acting Deputy Secretary highlighting weaknesses that were found in DOC's program. Further, a 2010 Department of Transportation (DOT) OIG audit revealed timeliness and internal control issues in the agency's suspension and debarment activities. In a presentation about this audit at the Working Group's suspension and debarment workshop last year, DOT OIG noted that continuous and open communication with the agency helped auditors develop realistic recommendations and avoided surprises when draft products were issued. The agency concurred with the OIG and initiated action to address the various recommendations.[36] Another example includes Department of Housing and Urban Development (HUD) OIG's recent inspection of the Compliance Division in HUD's Departmental Enforcement Center, the division responsible for drafting suspension and proposed debarment notices. Also, in response to the survey, one OIG explained that it learned through an investigation that its agency lacked suspension or debarment procedures; the agency adopted procedures after the OIG raised this issue. Several responding OIGs also advised that they were auditing or reviewing their agency's suspension and debarment practices or planned to do so.

Using Investigative, Audit, and Inspection Reports to Identify Suspension and Debarment Candidates

Several OIGs -- SBA, DHS, DOI and DCIS[37] -- assign someone to periodically review all OIG investigative, audit, and inspection reports for convictions, pleas, and other information that might merit suspension or debarment consideration.[38] If information that would support such action is found, a designated office within OIG then makes a formal referral to the agency. Other OIGs provide reports of indictments, convictions, or other court actions to the agency offices responsible for suspension and debarment determinations. Sometimes this may involve reaching out to the relevant investigator to obtain copies of indictments and/or criminal judgments before making the referral to the SDO. IG offices providing such reports include the OIGs for Department of Agriculture, Tennessee Valley Authority, HUD, Social Security Administration, and EPA.

Evaluation of Suspension and Debarment Referrals (Nov. 4, 2010), http://www.hudoig.gov/pdf/IEReports/IED-11-001R.pdf.

[36] DOT OIG presented an overview of the audit process and a summary of these findings at the Working Group's workshop in October 2010. That presentation can be found at: http://www.nsf.gov/oig/SD2010.jsp. A copy of the audit report is at: http://www.oig.dot.gov/library-item/5296.

[37] The Defense Criminal Investigative Service (DCIS) is a component of the Department of Defense Office of Inspector General.

[38] It is worth note that civil actions (including qui tam complaints under the False Claims Act) can also provide evidence for suspension and debarment referrals.

Possible Enhancements to OIG Referral Practices

Regular Consideration of Possible Referrals

The use of suspension and debarment might also be increased through measures designed to encourage OIG employees to make a referral whenever evidence indicates that doing so may be warranted. Approximately 44% of OIG survey respondents reported that they use methods such as statistics (pertaining to numbers of referrals) to encourage investigators and/or auditors to consider using suspension and debarment in appropriate circumstances. For example, one OIG requires that cases be referred for suspension or debarment within seven days of an indictment or conviction, and its agents are encouraged to make fact-based suspension or debarment referrals when warranted by available evidence. DOJ OIG recently issued guidance that places a "high priority" on field managers to report on cases where suspension and debarment might be viable remedies and to provide periodic updates to headquarters on such cases' status. Another unidentified office reported that an OIG Bulletin requires investigative regions to refer to the agency all subjects that are charged via criminal complaint, indictment, or information for possible suspension, and to refer all subjects that are sentenced for possible debarment.

One OIG reported that statistics on debarments and suspensions are recorded and evaluated during performance appraisals and another advised that investigators receive "statistical credit for suspensions and debarments." DCIS reported that it issues annual investigative priorities, goals, and objectives, which place an increased emphasis upon coordination of remedies, including suspension and debarment. Several OIGs stated that they have policies or practices that include a suspension and debarment assessment as part of their office of investigation's ongoing case review process. As such, we note that, rather than serving as a performance metric, suspension and debarment statistics could simply illustrate the extent to which employees have considered these remedies as part of their audit or investigative work. Many offices also generally reported that they encourage investigators, and in some cases auditors and inspectors, to identify and refer appropriate cases for suspension and debarment. OIGs might wish to consider these or other methods to require or encourage employees to identify and make well-supported suspension and debarment referrals.

Dedicated Efforts in Preparing and Tracking Referrals

Establishing a systematic process for preparing and tracking OIG suspension and debarment referrals, including the use of referral templates and checklists (tailored for investigative and non-investigative referrals), is another means OIGs have used to facilitate suspension and debarment actions. The SBA OIG Counsel Division, for example, in coordination with the Investigations Division, prepares detailed suspension and debarment recommendation packages, including a proposed notice of debarment or suspension setting forth the relevant facts, and a tabbed index of evidentiary materials.[39] In addition, SBA OIG has developed a routing form to facilitate the agency's consideration of recommendations, and simultaneously transmits recommendation packages to both the agency SDO and the Office of General Counsel. This practice has resulted in quicker turn-around times for debarments and encouraged SBA's use of pre-indictment suspensions. SBA OIG's referral form is attached at Appendix B.

DOJ OIG's Investigative Division and Office of General Counsel work together to develop referral memoranda, coordinate with prosecutors as needed, and submit the referral memoranda and evidentiary support to the SDO. United States Postal Service (USPS) OIG's Office of General Counsel gets referrals from the OIG Contract Fraud Program Manager, prepares a formal referral memorandum, summarizing all relevant facts and setting forth the specific grounds for debarment, and submits the referral memorandum, along with an administrative record supporting the action, to the SDO. An example of a referral memorandum from USPS OIG is attached at Appendix C, and an example from National Science Foundation (NSF) OIG is attached at Appendix D.

Other OIGs reported that they have developed tracking systems to monitor the status of suspension and debarment recommendations that they submit to their agencies. DOT OIG, for instance, has developed an automated referral system that allows that office to make and track electronic referrals. SBA and NSF OIGs also advised that they have developed tracking systems designed to monitor referrals as they progress from OIG to the agency and through a final decision. The Working Group suggests that OIGs consider implementing routine processes such as these, as appropriate for their particular offices, in order to facilitate the development, submission, and later tracking of referrals after they are made to the agency.

Development of Strong OIG Suspension and Debarment Policies

Many of the practices discussed above are incorporated into OIGs' suspension and debarment policies, lending structure and organization to the process. According to the OIG survey, 59% of respondents have a written policy for handling suspension and debarment referrals to the agency. Most focus on offices of investigation and are often included in investigative manuals. Some offices indicated that their policies have a broader focus. No respondents' policies expressly included auditors, though one OIG noted that it has informal audit-focused procedures.

A particularly comprehensive policy is the one developed by DOI OIG, which describes the roles and responsibilities of both agency and OIG staff and provides for a program manager on both the agency and IG sides, each of whom is responsible for the day-to-day administration of suspensions and debarments at DOI. That policy also establishes protocols for identifying potential suspension and debarment candidates; drafting referral memoranda or notifications;

---

[39] In line with this, the Working Group notes that OIG legal counsel can play an important role in identifying and facilitating referrals for suspension and debarment.

tracking actions and handling post-notification procedures; and responding to legal challenges to DOI suspension and debarment determinations. For maximum efficiency, the Working Group suggests that offices distill their suspension and debarment practices into suitably comprehensive policies. As appropriate, policies and procedures should be focused on both investigative and non-investigative activities.

Increasing Outreach among Relevant Communities

Effective suspension and debarment practices require regular communication and collaboration among all parties involved: OIGs who provide information that serves as the basis for the action, SDOs (and other agency officials) who take the action, and DOJ attorneys who may be prosecuting parallel actions. Understandably, competing interests and differing perspectives among these communities can sometimes influence the pursuit of a particular suspension or debarment. For example, DOJ and/or an OIG might wish to wait until there is an indictment or conviction before seeking a suspension or debarment in a given case, perhaps due to concerns regarding information disclosure. A SDO might prefer to wait for convictions instead of pursuing purely "fact-based" actions, or might worry about the resources available to pursue fact-based referrals either from OIGs or other agency offices.

As mentioned, communication and practical experience can alleviate concerns or misconceptions. Through active communication and collaboration, the relevant communities should be able to pursue suspensions and debarments more often, more consistently, and more successfully.[40] All parties to the process should have regular dialogue to work through areas of mutual concern and to correct misunderstandings. For example, where agency Offices of General Counsel have taken an unnecessarily conservative approach toward the amount of supporting evidence needed in fact-based actions, discussions might appropriately center on the actual standards of proof required under the FAR or NPR.[41]

Also, as noted earlier, preliminary discussions between OIG staff and SDOs may be necessary to lay the groundwork for non-investigative referrals. For their part, SDOs must safeguard information they receive from OIGs, and confer with prosecutors about circumstances under which evidence relevant to a suspension or debarment may or may not be disclosed. DOJ should promptly advise SDOs in writing if a suspension or proposed debarment might impede a pending case. Cooperation and communication among the various interested parties -- bearing in mind that the remedies may not be used to coerce a plea -- will greatly enhance the Government's

---

[40] The Interagency Suspension and Debarment Committee (ISDC) can serve as a useful resource for suggested practices and the discussion of issues of interest to the suspension and debarment community. The ISDC's website is: http://www.epa.gov/isdc/index htm.

[41] "Preponderance of the evidence" (51%) is the standard for debarment (*see* FAR 9.406-2(b); 2 C.F.R. § 850], and a lesser "adequate evidence" standard (similar to probable cause) applies to suspension (*see* FAR 9.407-(b)(1); NPR § 180.700(b)).

interest in protecting federal funds. The Working Group notes that often the OIG, based upon its relationship with DOJ and with the agency SDO can serve as an important liaison to help promote communication and coordination between these parties. Along these lines, where an agency has not actively pursued suspensions or debarments, the OIG could encourage participation in the Interagency Suspension and Debarment Committee (ISDC). This would allow agency staff to benefit from the ISDC's experience and could facilitate a more robust program.

Additional Training Presentations

In addition to informal outreach and dialogue, formal training on suspension and debarment may help increase the use of suspensions and debarments. In this regard, OIGs should encourage wide participation (not only by investigative staff, but also by auditors, attorneys, and others) in the suspension and debarment course offered by the Federal Law Enforcement Training Center (FLETC), and in other FLETC courses that have suspension and debarment components, such as the grant fraud course.[42] The Working Group also plans to work with the CIGIE Training Director to identify additional courses that could be directed in this area.

Individual OIGs might consider developing and presenting suspension and debarment training within their respective offices and agencies.[43] More broadly, IG community presentations to various organizations with interests in suspension and debarment, such as DOJ and other groups would raise these remedies' overall profile and could lead to their enhanced use. As part of the Working Group's efforts, training has twice been provided at the CIGIE annual conference and has been given at the AIGI conference, and to the Federal Audit Executive Council. Suspension and debarment was also featured in a presentation to the Council of Counsels to Inspectors General. Other presentation venues might include the Federal Senior Management Conference and others like it. Similarly, suspension and debarment-focused workshops can be an effective means to educate a wide audience about these remedies.[44] In October 2010, the Working Group held such a workshop, which was attended by over 300 investigators, SDOs, attorneys, and auditors representing more than 70 federal agencies and OIGs. Because of its popularity, a second event will take place in October 2011. Finally, pre-recorded suspension and debarment training (which could be made available through electronic and/or digital means, such as a free DVD or an online video) presents a cost-effective way to reach individuals who are unable to attend live presentations.

Regardless of venue or format, all suspension and debarment training should provide enough basic information to facilitate those remedies' use under appropriate circumstances, and be

---

[42] Information about relevant FLETC training programs may be found on the FLETC website, http://www.fletc.gov.

[43] The OIG survey noted that some offices already present such training to OIG and agency staff.

[44] Presentations are at: http://www.nsf.gov/oig/Susp_Debar_WS/suspensionanddebarmentworkshop2010.jsp.

tailored to take each community's distinct perspective and unique priorities into account. For example, as with less formal outreach, DOJ-focused training must not only discuss how suspensions and debarments work, but also demonstrate how and why those processes need not conflict with successful criminal prosecutions or civil actions. Other misunderstandings that might hinder suspension and debarment use (such as those surrounding fact-based actions or referrals stemming from audits) could likewise be addressed where appropriate. Targeted, and appropriately tailored, suspension and debarment training could be developed and presented to the relevant communities at minimal cost but with maximum benefit.

Leveraging Semiannual Reports

Some OIGs have advised that they include statistics and discussions of OIG-initiated suspension and debarment referrals in their Semiannual Reports (SARs). Others might want to emulate this practice; reporting on their suspension and debarment referrals in their SARs could serve as an incentive for OIGs to take greater responsibility for suspensions and debarments at their respective agencies and for agencies to take action on referrals. In addition, SARs are an excellent tool to educate the Congress and other interested parties about suspension and debarment activities. Including such data in SARs may also illustrate and reinforce OIGs' commitment to seeking these remedies and their degree of success in obtaining them by, for example, highlighting the number of referrals made compared to those that were ultimately "accepted" or "declined" for action.

Conclusion

Suspensions and debarments are important tools in ensuring that the government conducts business only with responsible parties. These remedies might be used more frequently if the relevant federal communities understood them better -- an understanding that could be fostered through continuing dialogue and training. All relevant communities should actively communicate and collaborate to avoid misunderstandings and to work through areas of concern, such as those involving information sharing. For its part, the Working Group will continue to explore ways to raise the knowledge base and overall profile of suspension and debarment through targeted outreach and training within the IG and other relevant communities.

Beyond this, individual OIGs may wish to consider adopting some of the suggested practices discussed in this report to the extent individual circumstances warrant and permit. Those suggestions include:

- Dedicating personnel to focus on suspension and debarment matters.

- Conducting audits and other reviews of agency suspension and debarment programs.

- Pursuing referrals that may be merited based upon the results of externally-focused audit and inspections, in addition to those arising from investigative efforts.

- Creating incentives for identifying and generating valid referrals, such as mandatory consideration of these remedies in certain circumstances.

- Developing standardized referral templates and checklists.

- Incorporating suspension and debarment practices into office policies.

- Encouraging broad staff participation (among investigators, auditors, inspectors, and attorneys) in suspension and debarment training.

- Reporting upon suspension and debarment efforts in OIG Semiannual Reports.

Appendix A
Causes for Debarment

The federal government may debar an individual or organization for a variety of reasons, including but not limited to the causes below. See FAR 9.4 (48 CFR Part 9.4) and 2 CFR Part 180 for the complete list of causes.

- A conviction of or civil judgment for:
    - Commission of fraud or a criminal offense in connection with (i) obtaining; (ii) attempting to obtain; or (iii) performing a public contract or subcontract;
    - Violation of Federal or State antitrust statutes relating to the submission of offers;
    - Commission of embezzlement, theft, forgery, bribery, falsification or destruction of records, making false statements, tax evasion, violating Federal criminal tax laws, or receiving stolen property;
    - Fraudulently affixing a label bearing a "Made in America" inscription to a product sold in or shipped to the United States or its outlying areas; or
    - Commission of any other offense indicating a lack of business integrity or business honesty that seriously and directly affects the present responsibility of a Government contractor or subcontractor.

- A preponderance of evidence of any of the following:
    - Violation of the terms of a Government contract or subcontract so serious as to justify debarment, such as (i) willful failure to perform in accordance with the terms of one or more contracts; or (ii) a history of failure to perform, or of unsatisfactory performance of, one or more contracts;
    - Violations of the Drug-Free Workplace Act of 1988;
    - Fraudulently affixing a label bearing a "Made in America" inscription (or any inscription having the same meaning) to a product sold in or shipped to the United States or its outlying areas;
    - Commission of an unfair trade practice;
    - Delinquent Federal taxes in an amount that exceeds $3,000;
    - Knowing failure by a principal, until 3 years after final payment on any Government contract awarded to the contractor, to timely disclose to the Government, in connection with the award, performance, or closeout of the contract or a subcontract there under, credible evidence of:
        - Violation of Federal criminal law involving fraud, conflict of interest, bribery, or gratuity violations found in Title 18 of the United States Code;
        - Violation of the civil False Claims Act (31 U.S.C. 3729-3733); or
        - Significant overpayment(s) on the contract.

- A determination by the Secretary of Homeland Security or the Attorney General of the United States, that the contractor is not in compliance with Immigration and Nationality Act employment provisions.

- Any other cause of so serious or compelling a nature that it affects the present responsibility of the contractor or subcontractor.

The causes for suspension are substantially similar to the causes for debarment listed above with the exception that contract violations are not grounds for a suspension. For suspensions, adequate evidence -- analogous to probable cause – that the specific misconduct took place and an immediate need for action are required. An Indictment or Information, or absent these, factual information meeting the evidentiary standard, establishes cause for suspension.

Appendix B
SBA OIG Referral Form

The SBA OIG reports that it developed this form to expedite suspension and debarment referrals to the agency. The office sends this form along with a proposed suspension or debarment notice setting forth the facts and regulatory grounds underlying the debarment or suspension and a tabbed appendix of relevant factual documents to the appropriate debarment and suspension official and Office of General Counsel attorney.

SUSPENSION/DEBARMENT RECOMMENDATIONS

Recommended Action:	Suspension Debarment Both
Submitted To:	___ SBA Debarment Official for Financial Assistance Programs ___ SBA Debarment Official for All Other Programs
Parties Affected, Mailing Address(es), and DOB:	(identify individual(s) and or business(es) to be suspended and/or debarred)
Background:	Discuss or refer to attachments
Basis for Action:	___ indictment/information (Attach copy of indictment or information) ___ guilty plea/conviction (Attach copy of indictment or information, plea agreement (if applicable) and sentencing document) ___ civil judgment (Attach copy of judgment) ___ other ground: _____ (Attach relevant supporting documentation)
Regulatory Basis for Proposed Debarment:	___ Federal Acquisition Regulations (48 CFR Subpart 9.4) ___ Conviction of or civil judgment for commission of fraud or a criminal offense in connection with— (i) Obtaining; (ii) Attempting to obtain; or (iii) Performing a public contract or subcontract. 48 CFR 9.406-2(a). ___ Nonprocurement Debarment Regulations (2 CFR Parts 180 and 2700) ___ Conviction of or civil judgment for-- ___ (1) Commission of fraud or a criminal offense in connection with obtaining, attempting to obtain, or performing a public or private agreement or transaction; ___ (2) Commission of embezzlement, theft, forgery, bribery, falsification or destruction of records, making false statements, tax evasion, receiving stolen property, making false claims, or obstruction of justice; or ___ (3) Commission of any other offense indicating a lack of business integrity or business honesty that seriously and directly affects your present responsibility. 2 CFR 180.800(a). ___ Other Ground (discuss below) Comments:

Regulatory Basis for Proposed Suspension: Regulatory Basis for Proposed Suspension:	__ Federal Acquisition Regulations (48 CFR Subpart 9.4) __ Commission of fraud or a criminal offense in connection with— (i) Obtaining; (ii) Attempting to obtain; or (iii) Performing a public contract or subcontract. 48 CFR 9.407-2(a)(1). __ Nonprocurement Suspension Regulations (2 CFR Parts 180 and 2700) __ (a) There exists an indictment for, or other adequate evidence to suspect, an offense listed under Sec. 180.800(a), or __ (b) There exists adequate evidence to suspect any other cause for debarment listed under Sec. 180.800(b) through (d). 2 CFR 180.700. __ Other Ground (discuss below) Comments (Include discussion of why immediate action is necessary to protect the public interest):
Imputation of Conduct	Is Conduct of One Party Being Imputed to Another Yes: ___ No: ___ If yes, discuss basis:
Recommended period of debarment:	(identify recommended period of suspension or debarment)
Other Information or Comments:	
OIG -- Review & Approval of Recommendations (sign & date)	_____ XXXXX, Counsel to the Inspector General
	_____ XXXXX, Assistant Inspector General for Investigations
OGC Legal Sufficiency Review (sign & date):	_____ Reviewing Attorney (Print Name:) Comments/Opinion attached: __Yes __No
Suspending or Debarring Official Review & Approval (sign & date):	_____ Suspending or Debarring Official ( )
List Attachment(s):	(identify documents attached to this recommendation)

DATE

MEMORANDUM FOR ███████████████, VICE PRESIDENT, SUPPLY
MANAGEMENT

FROM: ██████████
             Senior Attorney, Office of General Counsel

SUBJECT: Request for Debarment of ██████████████████

The U.S. Postal Service Office of Inspector General (OIG) conducted an investigation of the
above party (OIG Case # ████████████████). The OIG requests the Postal Service debar this
party for the following reasons:

1) ████████ pled guilty and was convicted in federal court of Theft of Public Money
   in violation of Title 18, United States Code, Section 641.

2) ████████ operated a Contract Postal Unit (CPU) in Kokhanok, Alaska pursuant to
   a USPS contract. ████████ stole approximately $6,800 by collecting C.O.D. fees
   from USPS customers and keeping the money for herself. She also "borrowed"
   $5,000 from the USPS by issuing herself USPS money orders.

3) Her Theft is expressly enumerated as a regulatory basis for debarment.
   Furthermore, her misconduct demonstrates a lack of business integrity and
   honesty, and is of such a serious and compelling nature that debarment is
   warranted.

The bases for this request are elaborated below and in the attached supporting documentation.

Parties Proposed for Debarment

The OIG requests debarment of ██████████████ (SSN ████████████, ██████████████
████████████████).

Facts

███████ operated a Contract Postal Unit (CPU) in Kokhanok, Alaska pursuant to a USPS contract. As part of her duties, ███████ collected Collect-on-Delivery (C.O.D.) payments from USPS customers. C.O.D. shipments are commonly used in remote areas of Alaska where customers typically do not have credit cards or checking accounts. (Attachments 1, 2.)

On numerous occasions, ███████ collected money from USPS customers to pay for C.O.D. shipments but stole the money for her own use. ███████ stole approximately $6,800 in C.O.D. funds. (Attachment 2.)

The OIG launched this investigation after being contacted by the Iliamna, Alaska Postmaster regarding missing C.O.D. funds. The Postmaster had visited the Kokhanok CPU and discovered over 60 C.O.D. receipts, indicating ███████ had collected C.O.D. payments for the shipments. However, the C.O.D. funds were nonexistent. (Attachment 3.)

███████ gave two statements to the OIG. In her first statement, she denied stealing any C.O.D. funds. But she did admit to "borrowing" $5,000 worth of USPS money orders. Specifically ███████ admitted she issued five money orders to herself for personal use, each in the amount of $1,000. In her second statement, she again admitted "borrowing" USPS funds for personal use, but this time admitted to taking $6,000. She stated she intended to pay the money back, but "other things came up." The money was used to pay household expenses such as food, utilities, diapers, and furniture. (Attachment 4.)

In February 2010, ███████ was charged in federal court with Theft of Public money in violation of Title 18, United States Code, Section 641. (Attachment 5.)

She pled guilty to the crime pursuant to a Plea Agreement. In her Plea Agreement, she expressly admitted to stealing over $6,800 in C.O.D. funds. (Attachment 2.)

In May 2010, the court convicted ███████ of the crime and sentenced her to five years probation. The court ordered ███████ to pay approximately $6,800 in restitution. (Attachment 5.)

Identification of Causes for Debarment

The Postal Service may be debar the above parties pursuant to 39 C.F.R. § 601.113(e)(1), which provides that a supplier may be debarred for:

> (i) Conviction of a criminal offense incidental to obtaining or attempting to obtain contracts or subcontracts, or in the performance of a contract or subcontract.

> (iii) Commission of theft, forgery, bribery, falsification or destruction of records, making false statements, tax evasion, or receiving stolen property.

(v) Any other offense indicating a lack of business integrity or business honesty.

(vi) Any other cause of a serious and compelling nature that debarment is warranted.

Explanation of Causes for Debarment

As a preliminary matter, the parties are "suppliers" as defined in 39 C.F.R. § 601.113(b)(8) and therefore subject to debarment. A "supplier" is any person or entity who:

(i) Directly or indirectly submits offers for, is awarded, or reasonably may be expected to submit offers for or be awarded, a Postal Service contract, including a contract for carriage under Postal Service or commercial bills of lading, or a subcontract under a Postal Service contract; or

(ii) Conducts business or reasonably may be expected to conduct business with the Postal Service as a subcontractor, an agent, or as a representative of another supplier.

███████ provided CPU services to the USPS in performance of a Postal Service contract for several years. She has unique and specialized knowledge about the operation of a Postal Service CPU, such as contract administration and performance requirements, and Postal Service mailing and money order policies.

Based on her prior experience and knowledge, it is reasonably foreseeable she may conduct business with the USPS again in the future. For example, it is reasonable to believe she may personally act as a contractor or as a subcontractor. Also, it is reasonable to believe she may act as an agent or representative of another HCR supplier by working on another supplier's USPS contract. Hence, she is subject to debarment.

The OIG requests the Postal Service debar this party pursuant to 39 C.F.R. §§ 601.113(e)(1)(i), (iii), (v), and/or (vi). ███████ was criminally convicted of Theft of Public Funds. She committed her crime during the performance of a Postal Service contract. Hence, the conviction is cause for debarment squarely within the boundaries of 39 C.F.R. §§ 601.113(e)(1)(i).

Even if there were no conviction, her underlying misconduct constitutes a cause for debarment pursuant to 39 C.F.R. § 601.113(e)(1)(iii), (v), and/or (vi). A preponderance of the evidence demonstrates she stole approximately $6,800 by collecting C.O.D. payments and wrongfully keeping the money for herself. She also wrongly issued $5,000 in USPS money orders to herself for her own personal use. She did so by engaging in a series of repeated, intentionally dishonest, and deceitful actions over a period of several months. Her criminal actions constitute Theft, which is expressly enumerated as a cause for debarment in § 601.113(e)(1)(iii).

Furthermore, her actions evidence a lack of business integrity and honesty, and are of such a serious and compelling nature that debarment is warranted. Those are causes for debarment under 39 C.F.R. § 601.113(e)(1)(v) and (vi). The evidence underpinning these causes for debarment consists of USPS C.O.D. receipts, her own oral admissions to the OIG, her written statements to the OIG, and the factual admissions in her federal court Plea Agreement.

Mitigating Factors

The factors set forth in 39 C.F.R. § 601.113(f)(1)(i)-(x) may be assessed in determining the seriousness of the offense, failure, or inadequacy of performance, and may be taken into account in deciding whether debarment is warranted. The evidence indicates ████ accepted responsibility for her actions by pleading guilty in federal court. She also partially admitted her guilt to the OIG, although she initially lied by denying theft of the C.O.D. money. Also, the evidence shows ████ was experiencing financial difficulties at the time of her thefts, and used the money for household expenses.

Explanation of Why Debarment is in the Postal Service's Best Interest

The decision to debar is within the discretion of the Vice President of Supply Management, with the concurrence of the General Counsel, and must be made in the best interest of the Postal Service. According to 39 C.F.R. § 601.113(f), if a cause for debarment exists, the supplier has the burden of demonstrating debarment is not warranted or necessary.

In this case, debarment of this party is in the USPS' best interest. As detailed above, ████ used the CPU to intentionally steal over $6,800. She took personal advantage of her position as a trusted USPS supplier, and violated the trust placed in her by the USPS. She also breached the sanctity of the USPS C.O.D. mail system. Hence, no reason exists to believe she can be trusted with USPS money or property in the future, trusted with the U.S. Mail, or trusted to honestly and ethically transact business with the USPS in the future.

Given her prior experience and knowledge, a reasonable possibility exists she might do business with the USPS again in the future if not debarred. Debarment will preclude her from doing so for a fixed period of time, and ensure she is not placed in a position to again victimize the USPS or its customers in the near future.

Request

The OIG requests the Vice President, Supply Management debar the above party. Please advise this office in writing of your final decision regarding this matter within 60 days of your receipt of this memorandum. If you have any questions or need additional information, please contact Senior Attorney ██████████████████████.

Attachments

1. CPU Contract
2. Criminal Plea Agreement
3. Case Initiation Documents
4. Memoranda of Interviews/Written Statements
5. Criminal Information/Court Judgment

[All footnotes in this example have been deleted]

Summary

The Office of Inspector General (OIG) has concluded that the Subject has willfully violated requirements related to the execution of an NSF award and has engaged in acts which are sufficiently compelling and serious that the Subject's present responsibility has been affected. The Subject's acts include:

1. her role in the filing of a Federal Cash Request misrepresenting the purpose for the draw down of NSF funds;

2. her role in the filing of a Federal Cash Transaction Report (FCTR) misrepresenting when NSF funds were spent;

3. her filing of a Final Project Report misrepresenting the status of an NSF award;

4. her actions associated with preventing NSF and OIG from discovering what had occurred and;

5. her role in the violation of rules and regulations governing NSF awards.

Pursuant to 45 CFR §620 et seq., we recommend that NSF:

- Send a notice of proposed debarment to the Subject informing her that she has been found to have willfully violated requirements related to an NSF Award, and to have engaged in conduct so serious and compelling that it affects her present responsibility;

- Debar the Subject for a period of 3 years from final disposition of this case;

- Prohibit the Subject from serving as a peer reviewer, advisor or consultant for three years from final disposition of this case; and

- Require the Subject to submit a certification that she has completed a professionally recognized course covering the proper administration of Federal awards.

OIG's Investigation

A. Background

On September 1, 2001, NSF awarded $249,509.00 (the "Award") to an Institution. In 2004, during the course of a proactive inquiry, OIG received and reviewed documents related to the financial management of the Award. This review, which included an examination of the Institution's General Ledger and supporting documentation, revealed that the Institution appeared to have spent over $32,000 in Award funds after the expiration date of the Award.

The initial term of the Award was from September 1, 2001 to August 31, 2002. The Subject, also the Principal Investigator, requested a First No-Cost Extension on the Award, which extended the expiration date an additional year to August 31, 2003. On August 29, 2003, two days before expiration, the Subject requested a Second No-Cost Extension. The NSF Program Officer denied this request on September 11, 2003, via FastLane. On September 15, 2003, the NSF Program Officer reiterated her denial in an email sent to the Subject. On September 16, 2003, the NSF Program Officer told the Subject again, this time orally, that "no new costs incurred after the expiration of the award would be honored by NSF" and also explicitly stated that NSF funds could not be used to cover the travel costs of a staff member then on Award-related travel (see Figure 1). According to the NSF Program Officer: "I stated frankly that [the Institution] would have to absorb those costs."

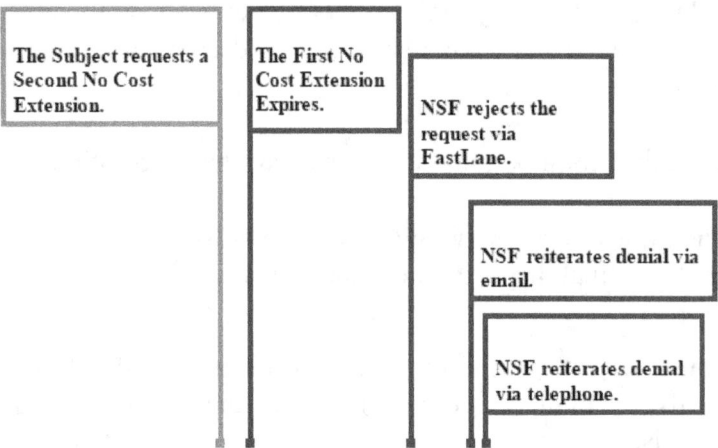

Figure 1.

B. The Improper Acts

1. The Federal Cash Request

On September 17, 2003, the Institution's Finance Director drew down from NSF the $32,247.11 remaining in the Award (Figure 2). In doing so, the Finance Director was following the instructions given to her by the Subject in a September 15, 2003 email:

> I was frantically looking for you on Monday afternoon. [The NSF Program Officer] at NSF (our program officer) rejected our no-cost extension request! *Can you pull down money ASAP to cover us?* (emphasis added).

To "pull down" the Award funds after the expiration date, the draw down was characterized as a reimbursement. This characterization was false; the majority of the cash request, $27,572.16, was not for expenditures incurred pre-expiration. Instead, the majority of this $27,572.16 constituted an advance for expenses yet to be identified, much less incurred. Over the three and a half months subsequent to the end of the Award, the $27,572.16 was spent by the Institution on items such as salary, travel and copy expenses related to Award purposes. The Subject approved these expenses and signed many of the Expense Reports associated with the post-expiration spending.

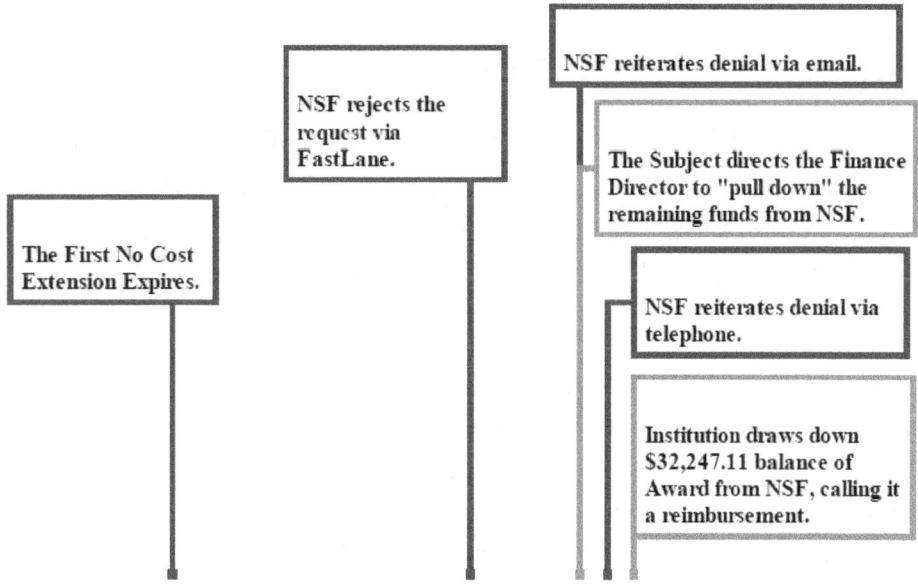

Figure 2.

2. The Final FCTR

On November 14, 2003, the Institution, via its Finance Director, submitted its final Federal Cash Transaction Report (FCTR) for the quarter ending September 30, 2003. This FCTR represented to NSF that all NSF funds had been spent as of September 30, 2003, with the following certification:

> (A) That to the best of my knowledge and belief, this report is true in all respects and that all disbursements have been made for the purpose and conditions (including cost-sharing requirements as stated in the NSF grant policy manual) of the awards.

This statement was false, in that as of September 30, 2003, all the funds from the final draw down had not been spent. This false FCTR served to conceal the actions of the Subject, and prevented NSF from exercising its reversionary interest in the funds.

3. The Final Project Report

On November 17, 2003, the Subject filed the Final Project Report for the Award with NSF, thereby representing that work on the project had been completed. Yet according to the Institution's own General Ledger, NSF funds were still being spent. As noted above, the Subject approved expenditures of these funds. By filing the Final Project Report, the Subject concealed this post-expiration spending and perpetuated the false picture that NSF funds had all been spent by the expiration date of the Award.

4. The Subject's Lack of Candor with OIG

No Knowledge of Award Expiration. In April 2005, during a meeting with OIG investigators, the Subject appeared to have no knowledge that the Second No-Cost Extension had been denied. On May 11, 2005, the Institution's General Counsel reiterated this in a letter and provided NSF OIG with a Memorandum written by the Subject disavowing all knowledge of the denial.

> I . . . do not recall ever hearing back in writing about this request. I have no record of our request being denied by [the NSF Program Officer]. Again if I had known that our no-cost extension had been rejected, I would certainly have halted all work on the project immediately. Absent this notification, however, [the Institution] continued its work on the project until December 2003.

In August 2005, OIG investigators presented the Subject with evidence that she did indeed have knowledge that the NSF Program Officer had denied the Second No-Cost Extension of the Award. The Subject did not provide a response when presented with this evidence and has never retracted her written statement.

The weight of the evidence does not support the Subject's May 2005 denial of knowledge. Specifically, there is a September 15, 2003, email where the Subject replies to the NSF Program Officer:

> Thanks for your note but I do need to discuss your decision further. The remaining funding in our project is currently covering [the Institution Employee's] time (he's currently on a TCUP visit this week), and we have already scheduled campus visits until the end of the year. Without this funding, [the Institution] cannot cover its expenses and, thus, fulfill its remaining obligations to the project.

Furthermore, the Subject's September 15, 2003, email to the Finance Director instructing her to draw down the funds also contradicts the Subject's statement that she had no knowledge of the NSF Program Officer's denial of the Second No-Cost Extension:

> I was frantically looking for you on Monday afternoon. [The NSF Program Officer] at NSF (our program officer) rejected our no-cost extension request! *Can you pull down money ASAP to cover us?* [emphasis added]

Confusion Over Expiration Date. In her explanation of the draw down, the Subject has stated that she was confused whether the Award ended on August 31 or September 30, 2003. There is some evidence suggesting that the Subject may have been confused about the date of expiration, at some point in time. However, other evidence refutes this.

The actual text of the Institution's FastLane submission notifying NSF of the First No-Cost Extension expressly identified August 31, 2003, as the Award expiration date. The First No-Cost Extension was submitted by the Subject. In addition, the Second No-Cost Extension, filed by the Subject on August 29, 2003, asks for an extension of *four* months, with the Award to expire at the "end of 2003." If the Subject had a good-faith belief on August 29, 2003, that the Award expired at the end of September rather than the end of August, the Second-No Cost Extension would have been for three months, not four. Furthermore, in an August 29, 2003, email to the NSF Program Officer, the Subject stated: "Our project is scheduled to end at the end of August." Finally, the text of the September 15, 2003, email to the Finance Director demonstrates that the Subject had actual knowledge of the Program Officer's denial at the time the money was drawn down. The weight of the evidence does not support that the Subject was confused as to the expiration date of the Award at the time NSF funds were drawn down.

OIG's Assessment

NSF has the authority to debar an individual who "commits a violation of the terms of a public agreement or transaction so serious as to affect the integrity of an agency program . . .." Such a violation occurs when the individual commits a "willful violation of a statutory or regulatory provision or requirement applicable to a public agreement or transaction . . .." Furthermore, NSF has the authority to debar an individual for other causes, including when a cause is "of so serious or compelling a nature that it affects [the subject of the debarment action's] present responsibility."

A. The Subject's Actions

Outlined below are the specific actions for which this debarment action is being recommended.

1. Filing a False Cash Request

As noted above, the Subject directed the Finance Director of the Institution to draw down funds that the Subject knew the Institution did not have the authority to spend. The only way to effectuate this was to characterize the draw down as a "reimbursement" for pre-expiration expenses. This characterization was false. The majority of the funds actually went toward unknown and unidentified future expenses under the Subject's control.

2. Filing a False Federal Cash Transaction Report

Additionally, the Subject, who served as the Principal Investigator, the Institution's Authorized Organizational Representative and a Vice President, was the individual who oversaw the programmatic and financial administration of the Award and thus bears primary responsibility for the submission of the false Federal Cash Transaction Report.

3. Filing a False Final Project Report

As noted above, by filing a Final Project Report on November 17, 2003, the Subject was representing to NSF that the work on the award had come to a close. NSF's Grant General Conditions require that an awardee file the Final Project Report within 90 days of the completion of the award. By filing the Final Project Report while continuing to work on the award and spend NSF money, the Subject was making a false representation to NSF regarding the completion of the project.

4. Failure to Tell Truth to OIG Investigators

The Subject's representation to OIG investigators that she was unaware of the denial of the Second No-Cost Extension or that she was confused when the award actually expired is not supported by the weight of the evidence.

5. Violation of NSF Rules and Regulations

The Subject's actions violated the following sections of the NSF *Grant Policy Manual* (GPM), the NSF *Grant Proposal Guide* (GPG), and the Office of Management and Budget (OMB) Circular A-110, all of which provide terms awardees must abide by when they receive a Federal award.

Section 251(b) of the NSF GPM (NSF 95-26) states:

> EXPIRATION DATE is the date specified in the grant letter after which expenditures may not be charged against the grant except to satisfy obligations to pay allowable project costs committed on or before that date. The expiration date is the last day of the month.

Further, Section 602.3 of the NSF GPM provides that NSF funds cannot be used past the expiration date of the award unless they are being spent to liquidate valid expenses accrued prior to the expiration of the award. Section V(A) of the GPG contains similar restrictions.

NSF allows the advancement of award funds only in very limited situations. Such situations can only occur when the awardee has an interest bearing bank account set up to receive the money, the interest from which reverts to NSF. The Institution did not have permission from NSF to receive an advancement of funding, did not place the funds within an interest bearing account, and did not return the interest funds to NSF.

OMB Circular A-110 Subpart C, _.28 provides that a recipient may charge an award only allowable costs resulting from obligations incurred during the award period or pre-award costs authorized by the awarding agency.

B. The Subject's Intent

The weight of the evidence indicates that the Subject knowingly and purposefully sought to retain wrongfully the remaining unspent portion of funding from the Award. Furthermore, the weight of the evidence indicates that the Subject intentionally sought to conceal and deceive the

NSF and OIG by continuing to mischaracterize the status of the award and by failing to tell the truth to OIG investigators. As discussed above, there is direct evidence of both the Subject's knowledge that the Second No-Cost Extension had been denied, and direct evidence that the Subject sought to conceal the truth from NSF and OIG.

Burden of Proof

In debarment actions, the burden of proof lies on the acting agency (NSF) to demonstrate by a preponderance of the evidence that cause for debarment exists. Here, the preponderance of the evidence indicates that the Subject purposefully and willfully violated the terms of a public agreement (the award) by violating the requirements related to the execution of it. In addition, the preponderance of the evidence indicates that the Subject intended to cover-up her acts by providing NSF and OIG with misleading and false information. The Subject has engaged in acts which are sufficiently compelling and serious to suggest that her present responsibility to manage Federal funds has been compromised.

C. Relevant Factors

The debarment regulation lists 19 factors that the debarring official may consider. Listed below are the factors pertinent to this case.

1. Harm Caused

NSF has a reversionary interest in funds unobligated at the expiration of an award. The Subject's order to the Finance Director to draw down funds remaining at the expiration of the award caused NSF to lose $27,572.16. By falsely characterizing the fund request as a reimbursement, NSF was left unaware of its rightful interest in the remaining funds. Furthermore, NSF has a significant interest in ensuring that the explicit instructions of its program officers' are not ignored by awardees. Here, the Subject's actions were in blatant disregard of both NSF award conditions and direct instruction by the NSF Program Officer.

2. Frequency of Incidents

The Subject's behavior included multiple wrongs during the period immediately following expiration of the award, and later, in her interactions with OIG.

3. Pattern of Wrongdoing

OIG has no knowledge of any instances of wrongdoing committed by the Subject unrelated to the award. Also, there are no known issues associated with the award other than those discussed herein.

4. Role in Wrongdoing

The Subject played the key role in the wrongful activity associated with the false Final Cash Request and the subsequent cover-up. At the Subject's behest, the Finance Director drew down remaining Award funds. The Subject was directly responsible for the submission of the false Final Project Report to NSF. Furthermore, the Subject committed these acts with full knowledge of their impropriety and after repeated explicit warnings by the NSF Program Officer that the award had expired and no further costs would be reimbursed.

5. Acceptance of Responsibility

The Subject has yet to accept any responsibility for her actions associated with this matter. Since the inception of this investigation, the Subject has contended that she was unaware that the Second No-Cost Extension had been denied.

6. Repayment

The Subject has not repaid NSF for the wrongfully acquired funds. However, without admitting liability, the Institution has settled with the Department of Justice. Pursuant to a settlement agreement, NSF will be made financially whole.

7. Cooperation of the Subject

Throughout the investigation, the Subject was uncooperative with OIG investigators. The Subject first met with OIG investigators on April 19, 2005. In that meeting, she denied knowledge that the award had expired on August 31, 2003. The Subject's subsequent written response confirmed her position. In August 2005, OIG investigators presented the Subject with evidence that the NSF Program Officer had denied the Second No-Cost Extension of the award. Subject again failed to cooperate with OIG.

8. Position Held by Subject

At the time the wrongdoing was committed, the Subject was a Vice President of the Institution, the Principal Investigator on the award and the Institution's Authorized Organizational Representative.

9. Organizational Action

Pursuant to the above-mentioned settlement agreement, the Institution has agreed to implement a variety of corrective measures, including training of its employees, the appointment of an ethics officer, and the adoption of written policies and procedures to ensure compliance with all applicable Federal rules and regulations.

10. Other Factors

There is no evidence that the Subject diverted any of the misappropriated funds towards her own personal use or the personal use of others. All Award funds appear to have been spent in the furtherance of the Award.

The other considerations listed in the debarment regulation do not appear relevant to this matter.

Recommendations

Consistent with the need to protect the interests of the public and the NSF, we recommend that NSF take the following actions as a final disposition of this case:

- Send a notice of proposed debarment to the Subject informing her that she has been found to have willfully violated requirements related to the NSF Award, and to have engaged in conduct so serious and compelling that it affects her present responsibility;

- Debar the Subject for a period of 3 years from final disposition of this case;

- Prohibit the Subject from serving as a peer reviewer, advisor or consultant for three years from final disposition of this case; and

- Require the Subject to submit a certification that she has completed a professionally recognized course covering the proper administration of Federal awards.

The Subject's Response to Draft Investigation Report

We sent the Subject a draft copy of the Investigation Report and all Appendices thereto in order to afford her an opportunity to comment. The Subject chose not to respond.

Appendices

1. NSF Award ▓▓▓▓▓▓▓ entitled "The Digital Opportunity Partnership: Linking the IT Industry with Minority-Serving Institutions."
2. ▓▓▓ General Ledger 12 Months Ending December 31, 2003
3. 7-25-02 Grantee Approved No-Cost Extension
4. 8-29-03 NSF Approved No-Cost Extension Rejected by Program Officer
5. Program Officer Affidavit: ▓▓▓▓▓▓▓▓▓▓▓ and accompanying emails
6. September 17, 2003 Federal Cash Report
7. MOI: ▓▓▓▓▓▓▓ Finance Director, ITAA
8. Subject's September 15, 2003 Email directing drawdown
9. Expense Reports Signed by Subject
10. FCTR for Quarter Ended September 30, 2003
11. All FCTRs for the Award
12. Final Project Report
13. MOI: ▓▓▓▓ Interviews, ▓▓▓▓▓▓▓▓▓▓▓▓ Subject's Memorandum to NSF OIG
14. Emails suggesting confusion on Award expiration
15. GC-1 Article 15
16. GPM Section 251, GPG and OMB Circular A-110 provisions
17. GPM Section 602.3
18. GPG Section V (A)
19. MOI: ▓▓▓▓▓▓
20. OMB Circular A-110_.28
21. GPM Section 441 on "reversionary interest"
22. Settlement Agreement between ▓▓▓ and DOJ